GW00992272

GETTING A PERSONAL WORD FROM THE WRITTEN WORD

Getting a Personal Word from the Written Word

by David A. DeLuca

XULON PRESS

Xulon Press
2301 Lucien Way #415
Maitland, FL 32751
407.339.4217
www.xulonpress.com

© 2020 by David A. DeLuca

All rights reserved solely by the author. The author guarantees all contents are original and do not infringe upon the legal rights of any other person or work. No part of this book may be reproduced in any form without the permission of the author. The views expressed in this book are not necessarily those of the publisher.

Unless otherwise indicated, Scripture quotations taken from the Holy Bible, New International Version (NIV). Copyright © 1973, 1978, 1984, 2011 by Biblica, Inc.™. Used by permission. All rights reserved.

Printed in the United States of America

Paperback ISBN-13: 978-1-6628-0377-2
Ebook ISBN-13: 978-1-6628-0378-9

DEDICATION

To my earthly father, Avery DeLuca,
who kept up personal communication,
not only with me, but hundreds of
students and relationships he developed
by working in several school systems.

Appreciation and Thankfulness

Thank you to my loving wife, Ellen, for her encouragement
and typing skills which helped to get this book from my head into written form suitable for
publishing.

Ultimate Appreciation and Thankfulness

To the Almighty and loving God before whom we will all bow,
but who in the meantime longs to communicate with us.

CONTENTS

Introduction: How this book can help us ix

Underlying Concepts, Genesis to Revelation 1
    How Do We Know It's HISTORY?

Getting a Personal Word from the Written Word – General Guidelines 3

Getting a Personal Word from the Psalms 4
    Studying the Psalms Study Page 5

Getting a Personal Word from the Written Proverbs 6
    Studying the Proverbs Study Page 9
    God's Wisdom in the Proverbs Questions 11

Getting a Personal Word from the Historical Books 12
    Studying the Historical Books Study Page 15

Getting a Personal Word from the Prophets 16
    Prophets at a Glance 18
    Studying the Book from the Prophets Study Page 20

Getting a Personal Word from the Gospels 21
    Studying the Gospels Study Page 23
    Studying the Parables Study Page 24

Getting a Personal Word from the Epistles 25
    Studying the Epistles Study Page 27

Getting a Personal Word from the Letters to Timothy and Titus 28
    Studying the Letters to Timothy and Titus Study Page 30

Getting a Personal Word from the Book of Revelation 31
    Studying the Book of Revelation Study Page 36

Getting an Overview with Song 37

Introduction:

HOW THIS BOOK CAN HELP US

Most people really want to learn what is in the Bible. They know it is by far the best-selling book of all time and that most learned men and particularly some of the giants in history have gleaned wisdom from its pages. Yet, it seems people begin a valiant attempt, make it through some of the interesting accounts in Genesis and Exodus, only to get bogged down in Leviticus.

Furthermore, they hear people saying things like, "That verse really spoke to me," or "I really sensed God speaking personally to me through my reading of Psalms," and it's easy to wonder, how did that happen? You don't want to doubt them, but what did they mean by saying, "I got a personal word from the written word." How do people do that? These inductive Bible studies are designed to help people do just that.

To get a personal word from each book is a little different depending upon which kind of book you are reading. Some books are historical, some are prophetical, some are poetry, and some are letters. We read each a little differently, and this book explains how to do that. It may be helpful to have an overview of the whole Bible as well as to see some of the key teachings that are woven throughout the book. We help you to see those things. It may also be helpful to provide key questions to guide our teaching of each type of book. You'll see those as you work through the individual study pages.

We encourage you to make copies of these study pages and use them in your own study and to build up a file of personal communications you have received from God.

You bought this book to help you do all these things, so let's dig in. Get ready and ask God to prepare your heart for what He wants to teach you.

UNDERLYING CONCEPTS
GENESIS TO REVELATION

T his is a diagram which gives the focus of three specific truths underlined in the Biblical record. The diagram is meant to underscore the fact that the cross weaves its way through all of scripture.

We suggest looking at each of these passages and reaffirming that these fundamental truths – **man is sinful, God is the sovereign Lord, and salvation is by the sacrificial blood** – are clearly outlined in each of the testaments.

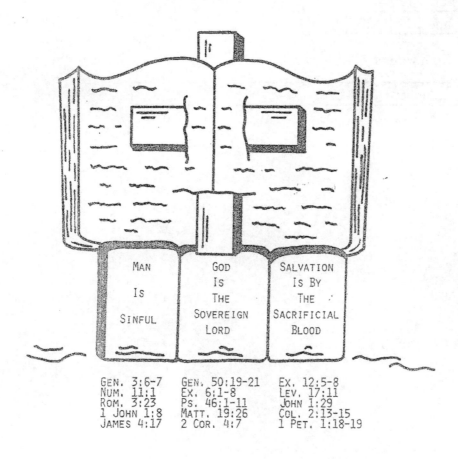

UNDERLYING CONCEPTS

GENESIS – REVELATION

MAN IS SINFUL	GOD IS THE SOVEREIGN LORD	SALVATION IS BY THE SACRIFICIAL BLOOD
GEN. 3:6-7 NUM. 11:1 ROM. 3:23 1 JOHN 1:8 JAMES 4:17	GEN. 50:19-21 EX. 6:1-8 PS. 46:1-11 MATT. 19:26 2 COR. 4:7	EX. 12:5-8 LEV. 17:11 JOHN 1:29 COL. 2:13-15 1 PET. 1:18-19

How Do We Know It's HISTORY?

It is also helpful to be reminded that this is "history." Many have said that history is "His story."
This piece reminds us of a couple passages which are almost proof texts from 2 Timothy 3:16 and 2 Peter 2:20-21. While many may question these, it is helpful to look at what Jesus himself says. These quotes affirm Christ's position on such controversial topics as creation and the lives of Noah, Jonah, David, and Daniel.

It is also interesting to note that books of the Old Testament are quoted in the New Testament, and the existence of genealogies tie the Old and New together.

  1. Specific Verses

2 Timothy 3:16	All scripture is inspired by God and profitable for reproof, for correction and for training in righteousness. (This referred to the Old Testament when it was spoken.)
2 Peter 1:20	No prophecy of scripture came about by the prophet's own interpretation. For prophecy never had its origin in the will of man but men spoke from God as they were carried along by the Holy Spirit.

  2. Testimony of Jesus Himself

Creation	Matthew 19:3-5
Noah	Matthew 24:37-39
Jonah	Matthew 12:39-40
David	Matthew 12:3
Daniel	Matthew 24:15-20

  3. Quotes from writers

from Isaiah	Matthew 12:17-21
from Deuteronomy	Matthew 4:1-11, Deuteronomy 8:3, 6; 6:16; 6:13

  4. Genealogies

Matthew 1:1-17
Luke 3:23-37

GETTING A PERSONAL WORD
FROM THE WRITTEN WORD

General Guidelines

How do you get to know someone? What changes a casual acquaintance into a close personal relationship? I suggest there are three basic things which need to happen:

1. You must spend time with the person.
2. That time must be spent primarily in listening.
3. You need to see the person in a variety of situations.

Many times, people feel a relationship with God will grow if they pray. This is commendable, but if you continually dated a person or met at another's house and you did all the talking, you would maintain the same perspective as when you began. In the spiritual realm, this means the words, "Lord," "Father," "Jesus," still have the same content as when you first heard them. There must be an ever-widening understanding of what it means to have God as a Heavenly Father.

Advice to people getting married used to include, "Don't marry someone until you have summered and wintered with him/her." The issue here was to see that person in a variety of situations. Be aware of how one relates to the other when the sun shines, when it is raining and when shoveling snow.

Many people grow in relationship with Christ as they see Him in a variety of situations. How does He react to children? How does He relate to the Pharisees? How does He talk to God the Father in the garden? What does He say to those who nail Him to a cross? This is a start, but God is unchangeable. How does God relate to Abraham in his walk of faith, to Joseph in the pit or in prison, to Moses in his disillusionment, or to the nation Israel as she walks in the midst of intimidating neighbors?

We want not only to see the songs God's people wrote (Psalms), the guidelines they lived by (Proverbs), but also historical accounts of how God has reacted (historical books, gospels, prophets) and related (other prophetical writings). That is what we are seeking to do in these studies. Your tools will be a Bible, a pencil, pen or marker, and some sheets with guidelines to help you ask questions of different passages.

GETTING A PERSONAL WORD FROM THE PSALMS

Since most people find it easiest to get a personal message from the Psalms, we will start there.

Songs seem to communicate feelings and attitudes better than almost any other vehicle. Melodies and beat often convey specific emotions. Consider the attitude difference between listening to "Zip-a-dee-do-da," the Gilligan Island theme song, "Sixteen Tons," "The Volga Boat Song." Take a quick minute to sing through those songs just to catch my point.

Now bear in mind we do not know the rhythm or melodies to the Psalms. They have come down to us in written form. They do, however, suggest tunes, and some writers have tried to pen tunes to fit with the word. The major thought here, though, is attitude, and we can pick that up from the words. For example, Psalm 8 and Psalm 9 seem to explode with trumpets and emotion of praise, while Psalms 10 and 12 seem to carry more of a longing that might be characterized more by long strokes on a violin.

That is what we want first to catch. Consider these questions and steps in looking at Psalms 27, 46, 55, 66, 73, 119, 139, and 145:

1. What characterizes his attitude? (When have I felt like that?)

2. What conditions is he facing? (How is that like things I face?)

3. What is his confidence based upon? (What does he know is true? What undergirds his thoughts and actions? What does he reveal about how God feels or acts?)

4. What does he call upon God to do? (Can I separate what is just venting feelings from what he really wants God to do?)

5. What course of action does he set? (What will he do, generally 'I will' or 'I' statements?)

STUDYING THE PSALMS

Portion studied _____

What characterizes his attitude? (When have I felt like that?)	What condition is he facing? (How is that like things I face?)	What is his confidence based upon? (What does he know is true? What undergirds his thoughts and actions? What does he reveal about how God feels or acts?)	What does he call upon God to do?	What course of action does he set? What will he do?

GETTING A PERSONAL WORD
FROM THE WRITTEN PROVERBS

Webster defines proverbs as short pithy sayings, expressing a well-known truth or fact. The purpose of these writings is given right in the introduction to the book of Proverbs:

> That men may know wisdom and instruction, understand words of insight,
> receive instruction in wise dealing, righteousness, justice and equity,
> that prudence may be given to the simple, knowledge and discretion to
> the youth—the wise man also may hear and increase in learning, and the
> man of understanding acquire skills, to understand a proverb and a figure,
> the words of the wise and their riddles.

All true wisdom comes from God, so what we are getting here is personal discussion from God about how to look at His world. It is genuine, earthy advice about how to deal with scoffers, loose women, a good wife. There are such practical helps as the soft answer (Proverbs 15:1), the things God hates (Proverbs 6:16-19), and some pretty solid warnings and promises.

That really is the heart of what God wants to say to us personally in the Proverbs. He wants to expand our vision—seat us in the heavenly places (Ephesians 2:6)—so we see from His perspective what is really out in the world. But woven throughout these warnings and blessings are some assurances we can rest in. For example, consider Proverbs 30:5, 6:

> Every word of God proves true,
> He is a shield to those who take refuge in Him.
> Do not add to His words,
> Lest He rebuke you and you be found a liar.

Just because of human nature we tend to spot that warning right away—do not add to His words—and there is also a consequence. The wise thing to do is to take refuge in Him. That is pretty easily spotted, but all of that rests on the fact that every word of God proves true. You see, if every word of God is true, then timing does not matter. Patience becomes an exercise in waiting confidently for God to do what He says. Again, it is grounded in the Word.

Consider these statements in Proverbs 5:18-21:

> Let your fountain be blessed,

and rejoice in the wife of your youth.
A loving doe, a graceful deer—
let her affection fill you always with delight,
be infatuated always with her love.
Why should you be infatuated, my son, with a loose woman
And embrace the bosom of another man's wife?
For a man's ways are before the eyes of the Lord,
and he watches all his path.

Here the wise thing to do leaps out at us. <u>Rejoice in the wife of your youth, be infatuated with the love</u> of that one whom God has given you. Yet here too there is a warning to <u>not be infatuated with a loose woman.</u> What is there here to rest in? It is that last verse. God knows what your particular path needs. He sees it all. That, according to the first verse, is why He gave you that particular spouse He did.

Now, because there are so many warnings and encouragements in each chapter, it is a little better to take shorter portions and really ask God to share His wisdom with you. Five basic questions guide our study to get a personal word from the Proverbs:

1. What predicaments that God's people encounter are described? The writer talks about ruffians, encouraging one of God's people to ambush others (Proverbs 1), the value of seeking wisdom (Proverbs 2), dealing with loose women (Proverbs 3, 5), diligence (Proverbs 6), elittling a neighbor (Proverbs 11). Decide what situation the writer is talking about and ask God to prepare you for these encounters.

2. Sometimes, rather than a predicament, the writer will talk about people. He mentions scoffers (Proverbs 9:7-8), a good wife (Proverbs 12:4), a hot-tempered man (Proverbs 15:18). Look at what kind of person is being described, and again ask God how you can best be prepared to deal with what you may encounter.

3. The heart of God's message concerns the principles that God wants us to know. He wants to tell us personally about the wise things to do and the blessings that result. You are really asking God to transform you by the renewing of the mind so you are not conformed to the world, but seeing things from His perspective (Romans 12:1, 2).

4. A second principle is the flip side of the first. You not only want to have God transform your thinking about what is right to do, but what is also foolish or harmful. So, the next things you want to observe are the wise things to avoid doing and the problems that result. Many times, these will be contrasted in succeeding verses, such as Proverbs 20:3: "It is an honor for a man to keep aloof from strife." That is the positive side, but right after that comes, "but every fool will be quarreling." In that same chapter, we read, "Do not say, 'I will repay evil.' Wait for the Lord and He will help you" (Proverbs 20:22).

5. This verse brings up the fifth area you want to look for. God has a habit of not only telling us what to do and what not to do in the Proverbs, but also giving promises of assurance. Here we see one of those: "He will help you." What He has said to do and not do is grounded in His promise of help. Such assurances are Proverbs 2:6: "the Lord gives wisdom;" Proverbs 3:25: "the Lord will be your confidence;" Proverbs 8:17: "I love those who love Me;" Proverbs 11:19: "He who

is steadfast in righteousness will live." What truths about God or life can a believer trust in? That is the rest that God wants you to have and those promises will be there. It is a great feeling to sense that He is personally speaking to you about them.

Try Proverbs 5:15-23, 6:12-23, 6:24-7:27, and 11:2-23 on the following study page.

STUDYING THE PROVERBS

Portion studied _____

Predicaments God's people may encounter (What situations that people may face are described? How are those like some things in my life?)

People God's people may encounter (How can I best be prepared to meet these people?)

Principles God's people should know: The wise things to do and blessings that result

Principles God's people should know: The wise things to avoid doing and problems that result
Promises God gives of assurance (What truths about God or life can a believer trust in?)

Key Proverbs to memorize for today

_____

_____

Application: How will living out these truths change your day?

_____

God's Wisdom in the Proverbs

1. What is the very best advice you received?

2. What Proverb, while it did not necessarily surprise you, did you read and say to yourself, "Wow, I wish I had read or understood the depth of that one when I was younger?"

3. What good advice have you tended to pass on to others either in the form of Proverbs or some other way?

4. When you read James 1:5 and read about wisdom, what definition do you think of?

5. How would you define a proverb for someone who didn't know what you meant?

6. Why Proverbs (Proverb 1:1-7)?

7. What are some of the characteristics of Proverbs? What do you want God to show you?

8. Suppose you saw or heard something about another person and you felt led to talk to them. What things would go through your mind? How could Proverbs help?

GETTING A PERSONAL WORD
FROM THE HISTORICAL BOOKS

A wealth of excitement, encouragement, and personal communication from God awaits the reader of the historical books. The treasures are there to be mined by those with the tools.

The key thing to remember in a historical book is that you are watching action take place. Feelings and emotions are not described in the same detail as say the book of Psalms. Principles are not often delineated specifically as in the book of Proverbs, but you do have real life depicted with nothing left out.

Books like Genesis, Exodus, Numbers, Joshua, 1 & 2 Samuel, Nehemiah, in the Old Testament and the Gospels and Acts in the New Testament are action oriented. There is dialogue, lots of action, and that becomes the key to getting the personal word from these books.

As we read the account, we need to establish in our mind a general view of what's happening. For example, in the case of Noah (Genesis 6:1-9:28) we see that the key elements include building something and keeping at it. The technical terms for these are faith and perseverance. To grasp what's here, then we ask several questions of ourselves:

1.   Are there any times when I'm asked to believe or trust God with little or no prior tangible evidence? (Remember it had never rained—Genesis 2:6.)

2.   Are there areas where I'm tempted to cease persevering? (Noah continued building 120 years—Genesis 7:6.)

3.   Do I find things that were said or revealed to Noah that fit situations I face today?

Those same questions help in reading Acts 1. As we read this passage, we see a sequence of events that is similar to different situations we face in our lives.

He presented Himself alive (1:1).	We are excited about new beginnings.
He charged them to wait (1:4).	We often have to wait.
They excitedly asked about the kingdom beginnings (1:6).	We eagerly expect quick changes.

He promised them power (1:8).	We get excited.
A cloud took Him up out of their sight (1:9)	Things don't happen quite as we expect.
They returned to the upper room and were praying.	We get down and wonder.
Peter stood up and said scripture had to be fulfilled.	God shows us what He's been up to.

Sometimes these historical books have significant dialogue, personal communication from God to His people. Examples of this would be Genesis 15:1-21, Exodus 5:22-6:9, Joshua 1:1-9. When looking at a passage like these, we need to hear those timeless promises that God has given to His people.

To study a historical book, we use the following outline:

1. The first thing we always do is pray. God opens up His truth to those who seek Him (Matthew 6:6, Matthew 7:7).

2. The next thing to do is read over the entire passage and get in your mind who the major characters are and what they're doing. A good way to do this is to underline subject and verb, possibly in different colors such as the following:

   The people lifted their eyes (Exodus 14:10).
   Moses said, "Stand firm" (Exodus 14:13).
   The Lord said (Joshua 1:1).
   I sat down and wept, and continued fasting and praying (Nehemiah 1:4).
   The people answered, "Amen, Amen."
3. Where do we face similar kinds of situations?
   What is it to have a "burning bush" experience?
   What is it to have a "Red Sea" experience?
   What does it mean to face a "Goliath"?
   Look for some overall patterns:
   Is God trying to teach people that He is Lord?
   Is God trying to teach people to have more faith?
   Are the people facing a discouraging, doubting experience?
   Does a prayer you read reflect truths about God which have been learned?
4. What does God say or do?
   Almost always there are statements such as God saw, God heard (Exodus 2:24), the Lord said (Exodus 1:7). When God speaks or acts it is worthy of note because His character and way of relating have not changed (Hebrews 13:8).
5. What practical observations do I make about the passage?
   This is where you take what you have read and apply to your life. Ephesians 5:10 says to try to learn what is pleasing to the Lord, so we use that as a guide and seek to note the following:

Promises I'm encouraged by

Love that I need to show more (Does it trigger a call, a visit, or something to do?)
Examples I'll follow (Do the major characters say or do things which ought to be emulated?)
Actions I'll avoid (Are there things which God warns about here?)
Sins I need to confess (Are there examples of statements or actions which are close to the way I have done things that I need to confess?)
Illustrations of Christ I'll remember (Are there things like the sacrifices of Isaac, the Passover, or the Tabernacle which picture Christ?)
Needs on which I'll take action (Does something I read bear prompt action?)
Gratitude that I feel for God (Is there something here for which I should be thankful?)

STUDYING THE HISTORICAL BOOKS

Portion studied _____

What are the major characters in the passage doing? (Look for verbs.) Are these positive examples to follow or are they warnings about how not to act?	Where do we face similar kinds of situations? (Look for some overall patterns.)	What does God say or do? (Look for verbs.) Are these timeless promises or warnings? If they are promises, highlight or underline them.	What practical observations do I make about the passage? Try to learn what is pleasing to the Lord (Ephesians 5:10).
			Promises I'm encouraged by
			Love that I need to show more
			Examples I'll follow
			Actions I'll avoid
			Sins I need to confess
			Illustrations of Christ I'll remember
			Needs on which I'll take action
			Gratitude that I feel for God

GETTING A PERSONAL WORD
FROM THE PROPHETS

Some of the most neglected books of the Bible are the writings of the prophets. Isaiah, Jeremiah, Ezekiel, and Daniel may be looked at to a certain extent, yet the reader who takes the time to probe the depths of Amos, Joel, Hosea, Habakkuk, and Obadiah is in for some real encouragement and challenge.

In order to study these books, the Bible student needs to pray and ask God for sensitivity in reading carefully. Generally, you will find a simple paragraph that describes how the prophesy came about. Here are some examples:

1. The vision of Isaiah which he saw concerning Judah and Jerusalem (Isaiah 1:1)
2. The words of Jeremiah (Jeremiah 1:1-3)
3. In the 13th year in the fourth month on the fifth day of the month as I was among the exiles by the River Chebar, the heavens were opened, and I saw visions of God (Ezekiel 1:1)
4. The words of Amos who was among the shepherds of Tekoa which he saw concerning Israel in the day of Uzziah King of Judah (Amos 1:1)
5. The word of the Lord that came to Micah of Moresheth in the days of Jotham…which he saw concerning Samaria and Jerusalem (Micah 1:1)

Now many people back off at this point and do not go on to read the prophecy. Instead, what we want to do is concentrate on five questions:

1. Who is writing? (Generally, that's pretty obvious from the book's name.)
2. Who is he writing to? (Watch for two places, Jerusalem and Judah. All the other names are "unbelieving nations.")
3. What is he writing about? (Generally, its either a vision of God or condemning some practice going on in that nation.)
4. What does the writer say first of all to those who would read it then?
5. What does the writer say to those who read it now?

To find out the answers to these questions, we break down a study into five basic parts, again asking several questions:

1. What are the conditions that exist in that society?

You can learn a great deal by reading carefully. Look for descriptions of what's happening. Some examples would be the following:

"They have rebelled." (Isaiah 1:2)
"Everyone loves a bribe." (Isaiah 1:23)
"They are full of diviners from the east." (Isaiah 2:6)
"They join house to house and add field to field." (Isaiah 5:8)

In some cases, it will depict an attitude:

"How long?" (Habakkuk 1:1)
"Violence" (Habakkuk 1:2)
"Why do you make me see wrongs and look upon trouble?" (Habakkuk 1:3)

We may not know exactly what violence or what wrongs are being described. (Any good commentary could fill in those details for us, but we understand those situations and feelings.)

2. What calamities does God say befall these people and why?
   Jeremiah describes what happens to Egypt (Jeremiah 46) and Philistia (47). Isaiah talks about Babylon (Isaiah 13), Assyria (Isaiah 14:24ff.), and Moab (Isaiah 15). The key issue here is why does it happen? In Isaiah 16, we're told it is pride, arrogance, insolence (Isaiah 16:6) for Moab. The issue is not so much who but why. These we can take as solid warnings:

   To avoid consulting idols or sorcerers (Isaiah 19:3)
   To not magnify ourselves against the Lord (Jeremiah 48:26)
   To not rob God (Malachi 3:8)
   To be more patient (Habakkuk 2:3)

In that respect, even in these seeming diatribes against the nations, there is a personal message for us.

3. What comforts does God give His people in the midst of world trials?
   One of the values of having writings which were penned in the midst of trials is to be able to find the encouragements upon which these people and people today can rest.

These encouragements or comforts are primarily in the area of what can happen in tough situations. Some examples would be the following:

   Isaiah 26:3 – Thou dost keep him in perfect peace whose mind is stayed on Thee.
   Isaiah 30:15 – In quietness and in trust shall be your strength.
   Isaiah 40:31 – Those who wait on the Lord shall renew their strength.
   Isaiah 43:2 – When you pass through the waters, I will be with you.
   Joel 2:25 – I will restore to you the years which the swarming locust has eaten.
   Jeremiah 29:13 – I will hear you. You will seek me and find me.
   Ezekiel 6:13 – You shall know that I am the Lord.

4. What truths about God are given in which the people of God can rest in confidence?
   These are primarily truths about who God is. It may be His attributes or some sense of who He is. Some examples would be the following:

   Isaiah 26:4 – The Lord is an everlasting rock.
   Isaiah 40:28 – The Lord is the everlasting God, the Creator of the ends of the earth.
   Daniel 6:26 – He is the living God…His kingdom shall never be destroyed.
   Daniel 9:9 – To the Lord our God belong mercy and forgiveness.

Isaiah 30:18 – The Lord is a God of justice.
Isaiah 37:15 – You are God, You alone.
Malachi 3:6 – I the Lord do not change.

5. What correctives are suggested to the nation or the peoples?
   The thing we are looking for here is what does God say should be done. All of the prophets give God's clear directions to believing and non-believing peoples. Some examples would be the following:
   Micah 6:8 – He has showed you, O man, what is good, and what does the Lord require of you but to do justice and to love kindness and to walk humbly with your God.
   Isaiah 7:4 – Take heed, be quiet, do not fear and do not let your heart be faint.
   Isaiah 8: 16, 17 – I will wait for the Lord, I will hope in Him.
   Ezekiel 3:1, 3 – Eat this scroll.

Please bear in mind that you read these books a bit differently and may not find responses to each question, but in general, as you read the book you will get a feel for what God is trying to say. Along the way you will see prophecies about Christ: Isaiah 53, Micah 5:2, etc., but more importantly you will have sensed some personal communication with God.

Here are some passages that may be good for practice:
   Isaiah 2:5-19
   Ezekiel 2:1-11
   Isaiah 37:5-20
   Isaiah 40:27-41:4
   Isaiah 55:6-56:2
   Haggai 1:2-2:9

Prophets at a Glance

Name	Date	People spoken to	World power	Biblical context	Old Testament References to the Prophet	Major message from God
Isaiah	740-680 BC	Judah before captivity	Assyria	2 Kings 15:1-20:21; 2 Chr. 26:16-32:33	2 Kings 19-20 2 Chr.26:22; 32:20, 32; Isa.	I can help even in the worse of situations.
Jeremiah	627-580 BC	Judah before captivity	Assyria & Babylonia	2 Kings 22:3-25:30; 2 Chr. 34:1-36:21	2 Chr. 35:25; 36:12, 21ff.; Ezra 1:1; Dan. 9:2; Jer.	If you don't get it together, you're headed for problems.
Ezekiel	593-571 BC	Jews in the midst of captivity	Babylonia	2 Kings 24:8-25:30; 2 Chr. 36:9-21	Ezekiel 1:3; 24:24	I am far more powerful than you imagine.
Daniel	605-535 BC	Jews in the midst of captivity	Babylonia & Medo-Persia	2 Kings 23:34-25:30; 2 Chr. 36:4-23	Ezek. 14:14, 20; 28:3; Dan.	I can demonstrate I am far more powerful even in national policies.

Hosea	755-715 BC	Israel before captivity	Assyria	2 Kings 14:23-18:12	Hosea 1:1, 2	Even though you abandon Me, I will still love you.
Joel	835 BC	Judah before captivity	Assyria	2 Kings 12:1-21; 2 Chr. 24:1-27	Joel 1:1	I can restore what seems like such a loss.
Amos	760-753 BC	Israel before captivity	Assyria	2 Kings 14:23-15:7	Amos 1:1; 7:8-14; 8:2	You better start getting serious about your worship.
Obadiah	848-841 BC	Edom before captivity	Assyria	2 Kings 8:16-24; 2 Chr. 21:1-20	Obadiah 1	You better care for your brother when he's down.
Jonah	782-753 BC	Assyria before captivity	Assyria	2 Kings 13:10-25; 14:23-29	2 Kings 14:25; Jonah	You better take My directives seriously.
Micah	735-700 BC	Judah before captivity	Assyria	2 Kings 15:32-19:37; 2 Chr. 27:1-32:23	Micah 1:1; Jer. 26:18	I am a just God in the midst of injustice.
Nahum	664-654 BC	Assyria before captivity	Assyria	2 Kings 21:1-18; 2 Chr. 33:1-20	Nahum 1:1	If you want to know I'll tell you, but it will be convicting.
Habakkuk	609-605 BC	Judah before captivity	Babylonia	2 Kings 23:31-24:7; 2 Chr. 36:1-9	Hab. 1:1, 3:1	If you ask the why questions I will tell you, but it will be convicting.
Zephaniah	632-628 BC	Judah before captivity	Assyria	2 Kings 22:1-2; 2 Chr. 34:1-7	Zephaniah 1:1	There will be destruction but also great blessing.
Haggai	520 BC	Jews after return	Medo-Persia	Ezra 5:1-6:15	Ezra 5:1; 6:14; Haggai	Quit using your resources on yourself and do what is right.
Zechariah	520-480 BC	Jews after return	Medo-Persia	Ezra 5:1-6:15	Ezra 5:1; 6:14; Neh. 12:16; Zech. 1:1, 7; 7:1, 8	Can you imagine how beautiful it would be to see Me glorified?
Malachi	432-424 BC	Jews after return	Medo-Persia	Neh. 13:1-31	Malachi 1:1	Melt the hard heart.

STUDYING THE BOOKS FROM THE PROPHETS

Portion studied _____

What are the conditions that existed in that society?	What calamities does God say befall people and why?	What comforts does God give His people in the midst of world trials?	What truths about God are given in which the people can rest in confidence?	What correctives are suggested to the nations or peoples?

GETTING A PERSONAL WORD
FROM THE GOSPELS

All that we have previously looked at will be utilized as we look at the gospels. The four good news or gospel books are Matthew, Mark, Luke, and John. We can view them like tires on a car or four legs of a chair. Each supports the picture of Christ in some way. If we are going to get a personal word from these books, we suggest the following:

1. It is helpful to read the particular book as a reader for whom it is written.

    Matthew writes primarily to convince believers in the Old Testament (Jews) that Jesus is the Messiah. He uses many Old Testament scriptures and talks about the kingdom of heaven and Christ as King.

    Mark is more like a snapshot album of Christ's life presenting Him as a servant. In many ways this writing is presented to the Roman mindset.

    Luke is more oriented toward the common man and Greek mind. Christ is presented as the perfect man.

    John presents Christ as the unique Son of God. The book is loaded with "I am" statements, and the message is presented to all mankind.

    As you read the gospels, it is helpful to understand which book you are reading, and what aspect or concept of Christ the writer is seeking to highlight.

2. Secondly, it is important to determine what your stance is. That is, are you reading for information, as an inquirer, trying to find out who Jesus is?

    The gospels are excellent for a person who wants to know who Jesus is. They are also incredibly encouraging for a person who wants to see how Jesus treats people, and how He reacts to adversity. So, there are a variety of personal messages that can be gleaned. For example, you can read the account of the prodigal son (Luke 15:11-32) and look at it from the standpoint of the Father (the one who keeps loving and forgiving), the son who left (the rebel), or the elder brother (the one who was jealous when his brother returned).

Of all the books in the Bible, these have more personal messages and variety of communication than any other.

3. Therefore, it is important to see the method of communication which is employed. To give you an idea what I mean, let me include some examples:

    a. Is it genealogy? (Matthew 1:1-17)
    b. Is it a historical account? (Matthew 1:18-2:18)
    c. Is it a sermon? (Matthew 5:1-7:28)
    d. Is it a parable? (Matthew 13:1-51)

    Let's take these one at a time:
    a. If it is a genealogy, we can ask these questions:
       (1) Why would the writer pick this type of genealogy?
       (2) How does it compare with other genealogies?
       (3) Are there any "peculiar" characteristics of this genealogy?
       (4) What message am I reminded of as I read it?

    b. If it is a historical account, we can follow the pattern we used in studying historical accounts.

    c. If it is sermonic, we can use the pattern we used in studying the prophets.

    d. If it is a parable, we need to ask several questions:
       (1) What took place before and after this parable Jesus taught?
       (2) What one major point is he trying to make?
       (3) Do his images have other historical precedents?

4. I have tried to include one "generic" form for studying the gospels. Try this out on these passages:

Matthew 2:1-18	Luke 23:32-38
Matthew 4:1-11; Luke 4:1-13	Luke 24:1-35
Matthew 6:25-34; Luke 12:22-31	John 3:1-21
Matthew 10:16-33; Mark 3:9-13	John 4:7-42
Matthew 13:1-23	John 10:1-18
Matthew 14:22-33; Mark 6:45-52	John 14:1-30
Matthew 22:1-14	John 15:1-17
Matthew 25:31-46	John 21:15-25

STUDYING THE GOSPELS

(Jesus is the bright and morning STAR)

Portion studied _____

STANCE	TESTING	ACTION	REVERENCING
What am I facing right now, and from what stance am I viewing this? What do I need for this day's activities?	What challenges come to Jesus or His disciples either directly or by implication in the account of the teaching? How do they apply to my situation?	What does Jesus say should be done? Or what does He demonstrate should be done?	What qualities of God emerge from this passage? How does Jesus demonstrate them or explain them and how can I incorporate those in my life?

STUDYING THE PARABLES

Portion studied _____

What is the setting?	What illustrations are used and what do they mean elsewhere?	What do the major characters in the parable do or fail to do?	What seems to be the one major point Christ is trying to get across?	What qualities of God emerge from this passage? How does the illustration shed more light and how can I incorporate them into my life?

GETTING A PERSONAL WORD
FROM THE EPISTLES

There is nothing quite as encouraging as receiving a letter from a friend. That is true for us, and it was true for the early church. These letters, the technical name epistles, came primarily from the apostle Paul, but Peter, John, and others also wrote a few.

If we keep in mind they are letters, it will be a key for us in how to study them. How do you read a letter from a loved one? There is little question that you sit down and read the entire letter at one sitting. Most of these letters can be read entirely in far less time than it takes to watch a television documentary, drama, or half of a football game.

Once you have completed reading a letter, what do you then do? If it's from a loved one, oftentimes you will reread certain parts to get the full meaning or at least to savor some of the encouragements. We do the same thing with an epistle.

One of the encouragements Paul put in one of his letters was the following statement: "Be imitators of me, as I am of Christ" (1 Corinthians 11:1). This is a real key for studying the epistles:

1. What is the tone of the letter?
    Some of the letters are encouraging. Some, like 1 and 2 Corinthians, are almost sarcastic in tone (2 Corinthians 12:11-13). It is very important to sense the tone by reading the entire letter.
2. What does the writer do or say to do?
    Many times, the writer of the epistles will begin by saying what they are doing, for example,
    I thank (Romans 1:8)
    I mention you in my prayers (Romans 1:9)
    I rejoice in suffering (Colossians 1:24)

3. What truths are those actions or feelings based on?
    If we read carefully, we find that the actions or feelings are based on solid truths:
    I am eager to preach, and I am not ashamed of the gospel. Why? It is the power of God (Romans 1:15, 16).
    I thank God, making prayer with joy. Why? Because I'm sure God will finish what He starts (Philippians 1:3-6).
    We comfort. Why? Because we've been comforted by God (2 Corinthians 1:3-4).
    Be holy yourselves. Why? Because God is holy (1 Peter 1:15).

4. What does the writer condemn either directly or by implication?
    As we read, we'll hear either specific statements or implied rejections of certain behaviors. Some examples would be the following:
    Suppressing the truth (Romans 1:18)
    Not honoring God as God or giving thanks (Romans 1:21)
    Having futile minds (Ephesians 4:17)
    Grumbling or questioning (Philippians 2:14)
    Minds set on earthly things (Philippians 3:19)
    Put away guile, insincerity and envy (1 Peter 2:1)

5. What does the writer desire to see?
    Often this will be in the form of a prayer, other times just in a statement:
    Let not one seek his own good, but the good of his neighbor (1 Corinthians 10:24).
    You may know what is the hope to which He has called you (Ephesians 1:18b).
    Walk in the light as He is in the light (1 John 1:7).

6. What truths about God are revealed?
    God is light (1 John 1:5).
    He is before all things (Colossians 1:17).
    God who is rich in mercy (Ephesians 2:4).

If we follow Paul's admonition, then his actions become our actions. What he bases those actions upon becomes our basis for hope. What he condemns becomes what we avoid. What the writer prays for and desires to see in people is what we look at as priorities.

A few passages which will give a "feel" for this kind of study are the following:

Romans 1:15-25
1 Corinthians 12:12-26
2 Corinthians 5:6-20
Ephesians 1:15-2:10
Ephesians 4:17-5:2
Philippians 1:3-11
Philippians 3:12-21
Colossians 3:12-17
1 Thessalonians 2:1-12
1 Peter 1:13-2:2
1 John 3:11-21

STUDYING THE EPISTLES

Portion studied _____

What is the tone of this letter?	What does the writer do or say to do?	What underlying truths are those actions or feelings based upon?	What does the writer condemn or say not to do?	What does the writer want to see? What specifics does he pray for?	What truths about God are revealed?

GETTING A PERSONAL WORD
FROM THE LETTERS TO TIMOTHY AND TITUS

The letters to Timothy and Titus are some of the most personal communications because each was addressed to one specific person. That specific person has been called to the task of shepherding a group of people. It has specific encouragements for the person seeking to work with a group of people. This could include the politician, the husband and wife in a home, a Sunday school teacher, club leader, supervisor, teacher, etc. There are really some very helpful principles of administration and supervision and things people deal with. They can all be found by the person who is patiently willing to dig a little.

Once again, it helps us to pray and read the letter completely. As we read the letter in its entirety, we see that it's written from a friend to a friend and from an experienced veteran to the willing learner.

After we've done this, we can begin to ask some questions of the passage to help see its immediate relevance to the situations with which we are dealing:

1. What conditions, situations, or people who work with people find themselves dealing with?

    These will fall into two basic categories:
    a. Things within myself. Paul mentions such things as timidity (2 Timothy 1:7, 8), tendency to dispute (2 Timothy 2:14, 16), impatience (2 Timothy 4:2).

    b. Things that are happening in lives of those we work with:
    People who reject conscience (1 Timothy 1:19)
    People who are greedy for gain (1 Timothy 3:8)
    People who are gossips and busybodies (1 Timothy 5:13)
    People who had a morbid craving for controversy and disputes (1 Timothy 6:4)
    People who revel in godless chatter (1 Timothy 6:20, 21)
    People who hold a form of religion but deny the real power (2 Timothy 3:5)

    Obviously, many times these will overlap. We'll find ourselves doing any one of these same things or manifesting these same attitudes, but that is the beauty of Bible study.

2. What qualities are people who serve supposed to aim at?

    Such things as these emerge:
    Love that issues from a pure heart (1 Timothy 1:5)

Harmonious marriages (1 Timothy 3:2, 12)
Hope set on the living God (1 Timothy 4:10)
Clear conscience (2 Timothy 1:3)
Confidence to know what you believe (2 Timothy 1:12)
Endurance (2 Timothy 2:12)
Hospitable (2 Timothy 1:8)
Holding firmly to the word (Titus 1:9)

3. What characteristics about God are emphasized?

Here we'll find such things as:
The strength in Christ (1 Timothy 1:12)
His mercy and grace (1 Timothy 1:13, 14, 16)
God did not give us a spirit of timidity (2 Timothy 1:7)

4. What confidences are given in which the servant of God can rest?

Here we will find such things as:

Life in Christ Jesus (2 Timothy 1:1)
God's ability to grant understanding (2 Timothy 2:7)
The goodness of creation (1 Timothy 4:4)
The folly will be plain to all (2 Timothy 3:9)
Good deeds cannot remain hidden (1 Timothy 5:25)

5. What course of action is advised?

Based on these confidences, what are we to do ourselves or be encouraging others to do? Here is where Timothy and Titus really give some specifics:

Fan into flame the faith in you (2 Timothy 1:6)
Be willing to share suffering (2 Timothy 1:8)
Teach faithful person who will teach others (2 Timothy 2:2)
Be unfailing in patience (2 Timothy 4:2)
Slander no one (Titus 3:2)

Several passages which serve as good examples would be the following:

1 Timothy 1:3-7
1 Timothy 5:11-23
1 Timothy 6:3-21
2 Timothy 1:1-15
2 Timothy 2:1-19
2 Timothy 4:1-9
Titus 2:1-15
Titus 3:1-11

STUDYING THE LETTERS TO TIMOTHY AND TITUS

Portion studied _____

What conditions will people who work with people find themselves dealing with?	What qualities are people who serve supposed to aim at?	What characteristics about God are emphasized?	What confidences are given in which the servant of God can rest?	What course of action is advised?

GETTING A PERSONAL WORD
FROM THE BOOK OF REVELATION

To many people, the Book of Revelation seems like a meaningless zoo…a puzzle of beasts and monsters that needs to be carefully deciphered by each generation. Yet, as we examine the introduction, we find that John says it is the complete revelation of Jesus Christ (Revelation 1:1). It ties together all the images, examples and teaching of Jesus Christ into one full picture of His nature, His work and His victory over the accuser of the brethren. At the same time, it is a reminder of His promise to come and of the grace He gives in the meantime (Revelation 1:4, 22:21).

Other than the letters to the churches (Revelation 2-3), the major personal word is a call for the endurance of the saints. This gives us His major purpose for writing the book. It is predominately a word of hope and a call for endurance to those who begin to wonder what's happening and why (Revelation 13:10b, 14:12).

The easiest chapters from which to get the personal word are two and three, because they can easily be broken down into several parts. The most distinguishing two words in the letters are the words, "I know" (Revelation 2:2, 3, 9, 13, 19; 3:1, 8, 15). Think what an encouragement it must have been to John, and is for us today, that God says, "I know," "I know," "I know."

We can break these letters to the churches into five parts:

1. What does God command?
   What does He say He knows that He's pleased about?

2. What does God make as an accusation?
   There are things God knows that He's not pleased about. Usually they are introduced by t h e words, "I have this against…"

3. What does God lay out as a promise?
   Usually this is in the form of an "I will" statement or an "I am" statement.

4. What is the remedy?
   What does God say can and should be done to rectify the situation?

5. What do I need to do about what I've read here?

Now to get the flow of the entire book, we need to ask some other key questions:

1. What is the situation in the life of the writer? (Revelation 1:9)
    What was happening in his life, and how would that make me feel? In fact, are there any parallels to situations I'm facing? This needs to be asked each time before looking at a section.

2. What illustrations are given and what insight do these give to Christ's teaching?

Is there some parallel in John's other writings or in another section of scripture, and in general, what do you think this revelation would mean to John?

As we read Revelation 11:1-12:17, for example, we find images and illustrations which are picked up from other places in scripture. What generally would these symbols mean to John?

Olive tree	Revelation 11:4, Exodus 25:1, Matthew 5:15, John 5:35
No rain	Revelation 11:6, 1 Kings 18:42, 45, James 5:17
Plague	Revelation 11:6, Genesis 6-12
Torment	Revelation 11:10; Matthew 5:10, 11; Matthew 10:16-26;
	John 16:2, 3
Ark	Revelation 11:19, Hebrews 9:4
Temple	Revelation 11:19, John 2:19-22
Woman	Revelation 12:1, Ezekiel 16:6-32, Isaiah 54:1
Bearing	Revelation 12:4, 5, John 15:4, Romans 7:4
Accuser	Revelation 12:10, Luke 23:10-12
Sand	Revelation 12:17, Matthew 7:24-28

In general, what do you think this "revelation" would mean to John?

John was probably asking that age-old question, "God, what are you doing?" (Revelation 1:9). God's response seemed to be, Don't put your mind on things outside that seem to be confusing. Put your mind on who I am, what I have done, and what I continue to do (Revelation 11:1, 2). I have always had a small number of witnesses. I have them now, and I will have them in the future. They will let their light shine as have Moses and Elijah (Revelation 11:3-6).

God continues by saying, Remember how I pictured Israel as a young girl (Ezekiel 16) grown to maidenhood. She has born some children (the church), just as you heard Christ pray (John 17:20). Right now, you don't feel the closeness of those people, and that word God is doing, but God prepares places for nourishing people in just such times. The angels have always been battling the accuser of the brethren. They have triumphed and will triumph by the blood of the Lamb and by the lives of those who give God their lives and don't try to hang on to them (Revelation 12:10-11). God takes care of His own, and besides, even though Satan may look pretty powerful, he is standing on sand (Revelation 12:17). Keep enduring (Revelation 12:10).

   Once again in Revelation 13:1-14:20, we see several "types" and concepts which are picked up from other scriptures:

Sea	Symbolic of the nations of the earth (Isaiah 60-:5, 57:20, Ezekiel 26:16)
Leopard	Symbolic of ferocity or vengeance (Daniel 7:6, Habakkuk 1:8)
Bear	Often symbolic of cunning, craftiness or great strength (Proverbs 17:12, Hosea 13:8, Amos 5:19)
Lion	Symbolic of rule, righteous or evil (Proverbs 28:1, Isaiah 31:4, Hosea 13:8)
Lamb that was slain	Symbolic of Christ as the perfect sacrifice (John 1:29, Isaiah 53:6, 7, Isaiah 40:11)
Like a lamb and spoke like a dragon	Matthew 7:15-19, 24:21, 24; Acts 20:29)
Deceives those who dwell on earth	Matthew 24:24-27, 24:13)

Mount Zion	Symbolic of God's rulership (Hebrews 12:22, Isaiah 4:4-5, Jeremiah 26:18, Joel 3:17)	
New Song	Symbolic of joy and praise (Isaiah 30:29, Ezekiel 33:32)	
First Fruits	Symbolic of multiplication (Micah 6:7, Proverbs 12:14, John 15:1-11)	
Fountains of water	Symbolic of life with God as the source (Jeremiah 2:13, John 4:14)	
Babylon	Symbolic of sin and spiritual adultery (Jeremiah 51:53, 1 Peter 5:13,	
	Revelation 14:8)	

Reap	Matthew 13:30-43, Amos 9:13
Rest	Luke 11:24, Matthew 11:28
Vine	John 15:1-11

God is saying, John, I'm giving you a timeless picture of what has happened, what is happening, and what will happen.

There have always been nations that arise intent on vengeance, acting with cunning and seeking to rule. The "authority" and power comes from the darkness. Don't be disheartened or deceived (Matthew 24:5-26). Yes, the cross seemed to mortally wound the powers of darkness (Colossians 2:15), but now I know it seems like no one can fight against this kind of intensity. I know you've heard God blasphemed and seen some saints die very horribly crushed. Right now, it seems like everyone compromises in some way and worships the one who said he'd be like God, but there are those whose names are in the true book of life for whom Jesus was sacrificed. God knows what's happening and what will happen. Keep enduring (Revelation 13:10b).

Listen carefully to what is said and done, because I told you false and powerful rulers would arise (Matthew 7:15-19) and deceive if possible even the elect (Matthew 24:21, 24), because they have such economic power that they can determine who will buy and sell.

But take heart, God still rules, and there will be joy and praise in following Jesus. Others beside yourself have been rejected man's way and been freed from the kind of tyranny you are experiencing.

There will always be eternal good news. Keep reverencing, trusting, and believing God.
Give Him glory, for the sin and spiritual adultery you see going on now will collapse. But be fore-warned, anyone who throws his lot in with this earthly, demonic, and unspiritual focus (James 3:15) will incur God's wrath and be disciplined severely in front of Jesus with none of the rest He promised. Keep on enduring. Real rest comes to those who die in the Lord. And Jesus will come to reap the fruit from His vine.

3. What encouragements toward endurance, steadfastness, and hope does God include?
    Remember that Revelation 13:10b and Revelation 14:12 say that this is a "call for the endurance and faith of the saints." As we study John's writing, we find many straight-forward encouragements that are woven throughout the teaching.

    I know – Revelation 2:2, 3, 9, 13, 19; 3:1, 8, 15)
    Worthy art Thou to take the scroll and open its seals – Revelation 4:11, 5:9
    Salvation belongs to God who sits on the throne – Revelation 7:10
    God will wipe away every tear from their eyes – Revelation 7:17
    The kingdom of the world has become the kingdom of our Lord and of His Christ and He shall reign forever and ever – Revelation 11:15
    They…conquered him by the blood of the lamb – Revelation 12:11
    True and just are your ways and judgments – Revelation 15:3, 16:7
    The Lamb will conquer – Revelation 17:14
    The Lord our God the Almighty reigns – Revelation 19:6
    I make all things new – Revelation 21:5

These words are trustworthy and true – Revelation 22:6
Let him who is thirsty come – Revelation 22:17
Surely, I am coming soon – Revelation 22:20

4. What is revealed about who Jesus is?
Woven throughout we find what John said we would find, "the complete Revelation of who Jesus is." We find these examples of who He is:

The creator – Revelation 10:5-6, 14:7
The all-powerful one – Revelation 11:17; 15:3; 19:6, 15; 21:12
Lion of Judah – Revelation 5:5
Lamb of God (sacrificed) – Revelation 5:6, 7, 12; 6:16; 7:10; 14:1; 17:14; 19:7; 21:9, 14
Bright and morning star (one who illumines) – Revelation 22:16
He is the Holy One – Revelation 1

5. What is revealed about what Jesus does?
Here are some examples:
He calls from the open door – Revelation 4:1
He sits on the throne – Revelation 4:3-11
He throws down the accuser with Michael – Revelation 12:10-11
He watches the beast deceive – Revelation 13:14-18
He judges the great harlot – Revelation 17:1-6
He destroys Satan after he has been loosed – Revelation 20:7-9

6. How will this affect my endurance, hope, and love as I walk today?

Here are some passages you could try for examples of this kind of study:

Revelation 2:2-7
Revelation 3:15-22
Revelation 11:1-19
Revelation 21:1-8

STUDYING THE BOOK OF REVELATION

Portion studied _____

What is the situation in the life of the writer (Rev. 1:9)?	What illustrations are given and what insight do these give to Christ's teaching?	What encouragements toward endurance, steadfastness, and hope does God include?	What is revealed about who Jesus is?	What is revealed about what Jesus does?	How will this affect my endurance, hope, and love as I walk today?

GETTING AN OVERVIEW WITH SONG

Oftentimes it is helpful to get an overview of what we are reading. These lyrics are meant to be sung to the tune of "Onward Christian Soldiers," a traditional and fairly popular piece of music. It is broken into two parts, the Old and New Testaments.

Onward Through God's Word
Tune of Onward Christian Soldiers

Genesis begins it all,
Tells about the fall.
Then the flood of Noah,
On through Abram's call.
Isaac, Jacob, Joseph,
God protects each one.
God cares for his precious children,
See Christ's work begun.

CHORUS
Onward Christ's disciples,
Trusting God is king.
Slowly we see Jesus,
Loving and leading.

Exodus moves on to share
Burden, grief and pain.
Children groan in bondage,
God comes through again.
Ten plagues show the nations
That the Lord doth reign,
Passing over cause of lamb's blood
Springing back again.

Moses reviews all God's work,
Deuteronomy,
All the care and patience,
Twelve tribes victory,
Jordan, Ai, Jericho,
Joshua given nerve,
Moving into Promised Land and
Choosing whom you serve.

Some tribes did not drive out all,
God still made a way.
Sampson, Deborah, Gideon,
Judges save the day.
Ruth stays with Naomi,
Where you go, I'll go.
Obed born to Ruth and Boaz,
Christ's Ancestors know

Hannah, Eli, Samuel,
Ark of God held tight,
We'll be like the nations,
Wealth and looks and sight.
God says, no, what's inside, friend,
Matters most to me.
God looks deeply on the heart
And not what's outwardly.

God moves to replace the choice
Men demanded so.
David slays Goliath
With a slingshot blow.
Jonathon's a faithful friend.
In the strife we see
Saul, David, Solomon,
Their years are 120.

Each king reigned for 40 years,
Then division came.
Ten tribes went to Israel,
Two tribes Judah claimed.
Nineteen kings served Israel then,
None were any good.
Twenty reigned in Judah and
Just 8 for the Lord stood.

Prophets sought to stem the tide,
Break down, plant and preach,
But only a remnant
Did their statements reach.
Israel captive from the land of Assyria,
Babylon carried off to exile People of Judah.

Cyrus touched by God to build
Moving in His heart.
Zerubbabel gives the
Temple work a start.
Ezra teaches, brings reform.
Then work on the wall
Start with Nehemiah and his people get the call.

God moves to replace the choice
Men demanded so.
David slays Goliath
With a slingshot blow.
Jonathon's a faithful friend.
In the strife we see
Saul, David, Solomon,
Their years are 120.

Each king reigned for 40 years,
Then division came.
Ten tribes went to Israel,
Two tribes Judah claimed.
Nineteen kings served Israel then,
None were any good.
Twenty reigned in Judah and
Just 8 for the Lord stood.

Prophets sought to stem the tide,
Break down, plant and preach,
But only a remnant
Did their statements reach.
Israel captive from the land of Assyria,
Babylon carried off to exile People of Judah.

Cyrus touched by God to build
Moving in His heart.
Zerubbabel gives the
Temple work a start.
Ezra teaches, brings reform.
Then work on the wall
Start with Nehemiah and his people get the call.

Onward Through the Gospels
Tune of Onward Christian Soldiers

Years of silence follow then,
400 is exact.
Silence then is broken,
God moves on to act

CHORUS
Onward Christ's disciples,
Trusting God is King.
Slowly we see Jesus,
Loving and leading.

Christ is born in Bethlehem,
Tempted wilderness,
Reaching out to preach good news,
Release and free oppressed.

Calls disciples to Himself,
Sermon on the Mount,
Woman at the well,
And parables which count.

Feed five thousand,
Waves rise high,
Followers quake in fear,
Jesus comes says peace be still,
And know I'm always near.

Pharisees demand a sign,
One that all can see.
Jesus points to Jonah
And to Calvary.

Peter asks how many times
Should someone forgive?
Christ says 70 x 7
If you really live.

Branches wave, Scripture fulfilled,
King on colt comes in,
But the cry "Hosanna"
Soon's "Crucify Him."

Those who looked for peace on earth,
Sickness cured and rest
Missed the point that in the "heart"
A person would be blessed.

Sitting 'round the Lord's table,
Do remember me.
Let this cup pass from me
In Gethsemane.

Prayed, betrayed, and tried in court,
False "truth" doth prevail.
Then denied and crucified
And splitting 'part the veil.

Grief and pain and anguish
Rule in every heart.
Christ is laid in a tomb,
Why did he depart?

Mary's travel to the tomb
And the angel said,
"He's not here…For He has risen,
Risen from the dead."

Thomas doubted, Jesus came,
Showed His hands and side,
Taught the truth of Scriptures,
Opened up their eyes.

Back to fishing they had gone,
Nothing did they seize.
Jesus came and said to Peter,
"Love me more than these."

Jesus said, "You will not know
When I come again,
But you'll be my witness
Unto the earth's end."

A cloud took Him from their sight,
Raised as God had willed.
Grieving, pained, they heard that scripture
Had to be fulfilled.

Peter's word at Pentecost
Touches every life.
Christ is part of God's plan
So was all the strife.

God had poured out all His love,
Though His Son was tried,
He's been made the Lord and Christ,
This One you crucified.

Onward Through
From Acts 4 to Revelation

Common men and confident,
Moving out to free
Those in Satan's bondage,
Prompting jealousy.

Murmuring over the food,
Pointed out a need.
Men were picked to give out alms,
Some from this task were freed.

CHORUS
Onward Christ's disciples,
Trusting God is King.
Slowly we see Jesus,
Loving and leading.

One of these, Stephen by name,
Full of power and grace.
Found teeth ground against him,
Stones thrown in his face.

When he said don't hold this sin
'Gainst these ones I see.
Saul of Tarsus stood consenting
Knowing it was he.

Later on he took a trip,
Breathing murderously.
God touched him while saying
Why persecute me?

He fell down, was touched with fear,
Said Lord I'll do all.

Used by God to write key books,
His name Apostle Paul.

Though the acts go on to share
All about his strife,
Sufferings he endured,
Those he brought new life.

The scripture goes on to give
Words to lift and build.
Other writings from some men
With Christ's Spirit were filled.

Persecution could not stop the work,
God still made a way.
John went on to Patmos,
God gave him words to say.

Thoughts of what the future brings
In that final hour.
Christ returns and deals with Satan,
Demonstrates His power

CPSIA information can be obtained
at www.ICGtesting.com
Printed in the USA
LVHW011129090622
720816LV00013B/257